RIGHT PLACE, RIGHT TIME

Lia Romeo

BROADWAY PLAY PUBLISHING INC
New York
www.broadwayplaypub.com
info@broadwayplaypub.com

RIGHT PLACE, RIGHT TIME
© Copyright 2019 Lia Romeo

Cover photo by Steven Roten

First edition: January 2019
I S B N: 978-0-88145-807-7

Book design: Marie Donovan
Page make-up: Adobe InDesign
Typeface: Palatino

RIGHT PLACE, RIGHT TIME had its world premiere on 22 January 2010 by Renegade Theatre Experiment (Artistic Director, Sean C Guzman Murphy; Managing Director, Cameron Gross). The cast and creative contributors were:

RICHARD LAMPARSKY .... Ron Talbot
GLORIA WINWOOD .... Helena Clarkson
STEPHANIE WINWOOD .... Elisa Valentine
LINDA MARTIN .... Blythe Thomas
MARK .... Keith C Marshall
BARTENDER .... Michael Daw

Director .... Aldo Billingslea
Production managers .... Cameron Gross & Jim Gross
Technical director .... Jim O'Sullivan
Stage manager .... Cameron Gross
Set designers .... Devin Berstch & Jim O'Sullivan
Sound sesigner .... Derek Batoyon
Lighting designer .... Carolyn Foot
Costume designers .... Tanya Finkelstein & Nina Harris
Properties designer .... Tunuviel Luv
Composer .... Rafiq Gulamani
Fight choreographer .... Michael Daw
Assistant stage manager .... Blair Baker

This production won Standout New Works Production in the 2010 Silicon Valley Theatre Awards.

CHARACTERS & SETTING

RICHARD LAMPARSKY, *40*
STEPHANIE WINWOOD, *28, very attractive*
GLORIA WINWOOD, *early 60s, very attractive.* STEPHANIE's
  mother
LINDA MARTIN, *40.* RICHARD's *ex-wife*
MARK, *mid-20s, tall, dark and handsome. Double-cast as*
  BARTENDER *(non-speaking) in opening scene*

The Waldorf Astoria Hotel, New York.
Time: The present, or something like it.

ACT ONE

Scene 1

*(The lobby of the Waldorf Astoria Hotel. 2:00 P M.
RICHARD sits in an armchair, dejected. On the table in front
of him is an empty gin-and-tonic glass and he is halfway
through another. He checks his watch.)*

*(GLORIA enters, wearing an expensive suit and lots of
jewelry. She surveys the lobby. RICHARD looks up, sees he
does not know her, and looks back at his gin-and-tonic.)*

GLORIA: Waiting for someone?

RICHARD: Um. Yes.

GLORIA: Your wife?

RICHARD: Um. No. My—my ex-wife, actually.

GLORIA: Wonderful. What are you drinking?

RICHARD: Gin and tonic.

GLORIA: *(To* BARTENDER*)* Two.

RICHARD: Oh, no, I don't think so, I've had two
already—

GLORIA: Have you been waiting long?

RICHARD: Yes—yes, a while.

GLORIA: Don't worry. It's on me.

(RICHARD *finishes his drink while* GLORIA *waits for the* BARTENDER *to pour two more. She takes the drinks and sits down in an armchair opposite* RICHARD.)

GLORIA: My daughter is getting married this afternoon.

RICHARD: Oh, that's—great, congratulations.

GLORIA: Thank you. We're finishing the preparations in the Grand Ballroom right now. Have you ever married off a child?

RICHARD: No…I imagine it must be difficult.

GLORIA: I've invited four hundred and fifty-eight of our closest friends and relatives. *(She drains her drink.)* It's a nightmare. Gloria Winwood, by the way.

RICHARD: Richard Lamparsky.

GLORIA: What do you do, Richard? Wait, no, let me guess. You're a doctor.

RICHARD: Oh—no.

GLORIA: A lawyer.

RICHARD: No.

GLORIA: An entrepreneur?

RICHARD: I'm afraid not.

GLORIA: My former husband was an entrepreneur. He invented the frozen burrito.

RICHARD: Wow.

GLORIA: And then he left me for a twenty-year-old shortly afterwards.

RICHARD: Oh—I'm—I'm very sorry.

GLORIA: It's all right. I've been sleeping around outrageously ever since. So, what *do* you do?

RICHARD: Actually I write novels.

GLORIA: *(Disappointed)* Oh. What sort of novels?

RICHARD: Uh, well, romance novels.

GLORIA: I didn't know men did that.

RICHARD: Most of them don't.

GLORIA: How about another gin and tonic?

(Beat)

RICHARD: All right.

GLORIA: Two more, please.

(The BARTENDER brings GLORIA and RICHARD two more drinks.)

GLORIA: You know, I don't read much, but Stephanie's an excellent reader.

RICHARD: Your daughter?

GLORIA: My daughter. The bride.

RICHARD: What time is the wedding? —Don't you need to be—?

GLORIA: Three P M. What time was your…ex-wife going to arrive?

RICHARD: She was supposed to be here at eleven.

GLORIA: I'm so sorry.

RICHARD: Me too.

GLORIA: Well, maybe there's been an accident. Maybe she's been hit by a car.

(RICHARD looks alarmed.)

GLORIA: Oh, I didn't mean really—at least I hope not—oh, dear. (She lays a hand on his knee, both motherly and suggestive.) You poor boy. Care for another?

RICHARD: Oh—no, I just started this one. I'm—not normally much of a drinker.

GLORIA: You ought to be. It's the best thing for a broken heart.

(RICHARD *takes a giant gulp of his drink.*)

RICHARD: You're probably right.

GLORIA: So tell me about your ex-wife. Is she very beautiful?

RICHARD: *(Honestly)* No.

GLORIA: But you're such a good-looking man. Surely you ought to be with a woman who's beautiful.

RICHARD: *(Blushing)* I—um—thank you. I—I met Linda when I was eighteen. And we dated all through college, and then we got married, and it was great—neither of us had been with anybody else, or wanted to be with anybody else—except—then—she did.

GLORIA: And you? You haven't wanted to be with anybody else?

RICHARD: Nobody else has wanted to be with me.

GLORIA: Richard, it was very lucky our meeting like this.

RICHARD: It was?

GLORIA: Yes. I've got something very important to ask you. But not here. Will you come up to my room for a few minutes?

RICHARD: Right now? But—you have a wedding in an hour—

GLORIA: Then we'll have to be quick, won't we.

RICHARD: Oh. Uh, well. All right. But what about Linda, what if she—

GLORIA: *(To the* BARTENDER*)* If Miss Linda arrives, please tell her that Richard is in suite 306.

(GLORIA *rises and exits.* RICHARD *follows.*)

Scene 2

(The living room of a fancy suite at the Waldorf. STEPHANIE, *wearing a wedding dress, sits in a chair sobbing. Her mascara is smudged and she attempts to wipe it with her veil.* GLORIA *and* RICHARD *enter.)*

RICHARD: Oh!

GLORIA: Richard, this is my daughter, Stephanie. *(She crosses to* STEPHANIE'*s chair and kneels down beside her.)* How are you, sweetheart. Don't worry, everything will be all right.

RICHARD: *(Uncomfortably)* Pre-wedding jitters?

*(*STEPHANIE *sobs louder.)*

GLORIA: Sit down, Richard, make yourself comfortable.

RICHARD: Maybe I should go—

GLORIA: I wouldn't hear of it. Stephanie will feel better in a moment. As I was saying, it's so fortunate that I happened to run into you. Stephanie is to be married, but the groom has failed to arrive.

RICHARD: Oh, I'm—I'm very sorry.

GLORIA: Richard, I want you to marry my daughter. *(Beat)* Stephanie, Richard is a novelist! Stephanie loves to read. And she's beautiful, too. Isn't she beautiful, Richard? *(She looks at the clock.)* Well, I've got to freshen up! I've got a wedding in less than an hour. I'll just let you two get to know each other a bit.

*(*GLORIA *exits into her bedroom.* STEPHANIE *and* RICHARD *stare at each other in silence for a minute. She makes an effort to compose herself.)*

STEPHANIE: I'm sorry about Mother. As you can see, she isn't exactly rational.

RICHARD: No, no, it's okay, it's okay. I'm—I'm so sorry about your wedding.

STEPHANIE: Thank you.

RICHARD: So, uh, I guess I should go.

STEPHANIE: You probably should. I'm sorry again. It was nice meeting you, Mr—

RICHARD: Lamparsky, Richard Lamparsky.

STEPHANIE: You wrote the "Tropical Midnight" series.

RICHARD: …Uh-huh.

STEPHANIE: Those were good.

RICHARD: You read them? Wow. I—I'm delighted. You're probably one of about six people in America who's read those books.

STEPHANIE: I thought romance novels usually sold really well.

RICHARD: Usually.

STEPHANIE: I do remember being curious what someone named Richard Lamparsky was doing writing romance novels. Did you ever consider a more…romantic-sounding pen name?

RICHARD: Yes, of course, but—well, I guess I wanted to be able to take credit, if I happened to meet one of the six people who'd read my books.

STEPHANIE: And you did. And you deserve all the credit you want to take for them.

RICHARD: Thank you. What about you, uh, what do you do?

STEPHANIE: Nothing. My father invented the frozen burrito.

RICHARD: Yes, I—I heard.

STEPHANIE: I just finished my doctorate—

RICHARD: Oh, in what?

STEPHANIE: Comparative literature. And since then I've been wedding planning, so…

RICHARD: And the man you were marrying just… didn't show up?

STEPHANIE: That's right.

RICHARD: That's awful. I—uh—I just got stood up too, you know. For lunch. By my ex-wife.

STEPHANIE: *(Confused)* Oh. I'm sorry.

RICHARD: No, no, don't be, it's—it's nothing. I just wanted to let you know I know how you feel.

STEPHANIE: I doubt that.

RICHARD: No—no of course not, I'm sorry. I have no idea how you feel.

STEPHANIE: Well, to be fair, I have no idea how *you* feel.

RICHARD: No, no, you were right, completely right, really, I'm…gonna go.

STEPHANIE: Actually, do you think you could stay and talk to me? Just for a few minutes? I need something to think about.

RICHARD: Oh—of course, sure, I'd be happy to talk to you.

STEPHANIE: Would you like some champagne? I hate to see it go to waste. It's very good.

RICHARD: Okay.

(STEPHANIE expertly opens the champagne and pours it into two glasses.)

RICHARD: What did you want me to talk about?

STEPHANIE: I don't know…tell me…tell me about your ex-wife. Unless that's painful.

RICHARD: No, no, Linda's not painful, Linda's…great, actually I don't know how she is, I haven't really seen her since we split up. I try to keep in touch, but she lives in Chicago now…and she's in town on business so I thought we could meet for dinner, maybe have a couple of drinks, but she only had time for lunch, and she told me to meet her here but…she never showed.

STEPHANIE: Maybe there's been an accident.

RICHARD: That's what your mother said. I hope not, I'd rather she just decided not to see me than she's hurt, or God knows what.

STEPHANIE: Really? I'd rather Mark were dead.

RICHARD: *(Taken aback)* Oh. Well. Are you sure he isn't?

STEPHANIE: He was supposed to be here this morning. If anything had happened we'd have heard by now.

RICHARD: But that just doesn't make sense. I mean who plans a wedding…especially to a woman like you…

STEPHANIE: I guess Mark does.

RICHARD: Uh—yeah, I—I guess so. What does Mark do?

STEPHANIE: Nothing. His grandfather invented the spork.

RICHARD: Oh.

STEPHANIE: I met him when we were both vacationing on the Riviera, and we spent a week together. And on the last night he asked me to marry him, and…of course I've had plenty of men who've asked me that before, but this time I said yes.

RICHARD: Why?

STEPHANIE: Well, it felt like the right time. I'd always told myself I'd get married by the time I was twenty-eight. And I was twenty-eight, and there was this lovely man, so I figured I ought to.

RICHARD: Why twenty-eight?

STEPHANIE: Because after that it gets harder. Everyone starts to wonder why you haven't done it already. And they start to think maybe there's something wrong with you, and then your breasts go this way and your hips go that way, and before you know it you end up like my mother, never invited to couples weekends or dinner parties because they don't want her to feel badly that she's the only single one there. So we set a date, and we've been talking on the phone, only the last couple of days he hasn't been returning my calls, and I called today and he's changed his number... *(She begins crying but gets a hold of herself quickly)*

RICHARD: I'm so sorry.

STEPHANIE: It's not Mark, really, I mean I hardly really know him. I'm just so embarrassed. Things like this don't happen to me, I always have my shit together... I'm sorry. I shouldn't swear.

RICHARD: No, no, you deserve to. Shit. Fuck.

(STEPHANIE laughs. Then she begins to cry again. RICHARD watches helplessly.)

RICHARD: Is there anything at all I can...do for you? More champagne?

STEPHANIE: Yes, please.

(RICHARD pours more champagne into their glasses.)

STEPHANIE: Could you stroke my hair? I know that's strange, it's just my father used to do it when I was a girl and it was so comforting.

RICHARD: Sure.

(RICHARD crosses to STEPHANIE, and strokes her hair, awkwardly.)

STEPHANIE: Do you want to kiss me, Richard?

RICHARD: *(Surprised)* Um. Well. A little.

STEPHANIE: Do you want to kiss me every night, and have me there when you wake up and kiss me again in the morning?

RICHARD: I—

STEPHANIE: And take care of me. I don't mean financially. I've got trust funds, and we'd live very well. But I've just been hurt badly and I need a good man.

RICHARD: I—I'm not a good man.

STEPHANIE: Well, that won't work then.

RICHARD: I mean—I don't know. I'm not a bad man. I try to be a good man, most of the time.

STEPHANIE: It's two-thirty, Richard. Are you or not?

RICHARD: I don't know.

STEPHANIE: I'll take my chances. (*She turns her face up.*) You can kiss me now.

(RICHARD *kisses* STEPHANIE.)

STEPHANIE: Richard, how often does something extraordinary come into your life?

RICHARD: Never.

STEPHANIE: It just did. If you want it, I'm sure somebody has a tux you can borrow.

RICHARD: What? —No, I mean—this is crazy!

STEPHANIE: No it's not. I like you, and I'd like to marry you. I've got a wedding planned in half an hour, so if you'd like to marry me too, then we should do it.

RICHARD: You can't just substitute one groom for another!

STEPHANIE: No one had ever even met Mark. We'll tell them Richard is your legal name.

RICHARD: But—

STEPHANIE: You've been married, Richard—weddings are all about the bride. The groom is just another accessory. The only really important thing is that you've got one.

RICHARD: But there are…legal requirements—

STEPHANIE: We'd planned to take care of the license and prenup after the ceremony. We have an appointment tomorrow at City Hall.

RICHARD: I'm sorry, Stephanie, but I can't let you use me just so you don't get embarrassed in front of your mother's four hundred friends.

STEPHANIE: I'm not using you that way. I'm using you the way you thought you were going to use my mother. (Beat) You did, you thought you were going to sleep with my mother. I figured you out as soon as you walked in. You'd been stood up, you were hurt, you were lonely…and there was my mother. An older woman, but still attractive, and you thought you could have her…and you needed that, that proof that even though everything wasn't the way it should be it was still good enough. (Beat) More champagne?

RICHARD: Yes, please.

STEPHANIE: You're good enough. I'm sorry it's not very romantic, but it's all I can offer right now. And I think—I'm pretty sure, to tell you the truth—that I'd be good enough for you.

RICHARD: But that doesn't mean we should get *married*, I mean you're beautiful, and charming, and—well—very unusual—and what if we, you know, went out to dinner sometime?

STEPHANIE: It wouldn't work. You can't go backwards, from a marriage proposal to a first date.

RICHARD: Marriage is supposed to be about love.

STEPHANIE: That's a nice idea, but it's a social institution. Sometimes it has something to do with love, but sometimes it doesn't.

RICHARD: You're too young to be so jaded!

STEPHANIE: I've always been mature for my age. Would you kiss me again?

(RICHARD *and* STEPHANIE *kiss. They are still kissing as* GLORIA *re-enters holding a tuxedo.*)

GLORIA: Oh, aren't you sweet. (*She holds the tuxedo up against* RICHARD) I got this from Uncle Alfred. It ought to be about the right size.

STEPHANIE: Could you go in the bedroom so Richard can try it on?

GLORIA: He can try it on with me here. I'm harmless.

STEPHANIE: Mother, please.

(GLORIA *huffs and exits into her bedroom.*)

STEPHANIE: I'm sorry.

RICHARD: That's all right.

STEPHANIE: Take off your clothes.

(RICHARD *drains his champagne glass, then removes his pants and shirt.*)

STEPHANIE: You have a great body, Richard.

RICHARD: Thank you. I—I try to work out.

STEPHANIE: There's a fitness center downstairs. I go every morning. (*Beat*) Try it on.

(RICHARD *begins putting on the tuxedo.* STEPHANIE *helps him.*)

RICHARD: How long have you been staying here?

STEPHANIE: We live here.

RICHARD: In the hotel?

STEPHANIE: Yes, this section's for private apartments. Mother and I share the suite. Isn't it nice?

RICHARD: It's gorgeous.

STEPHANIE: It was one of the best things Mother got out of the divorce. But you and I, we'll get our own place, once everything's settled. I've been looking at real estate on both sides of the park, though I like the east side better—what about you?

RICHARD: I—I don't know. I've never really thought about it.

STEPHANIE: Maybe you should.

(RICHARD *finishes putting on the tuxedo.* STEPHANIE *shows him the mirror and he looks at himself.*)

RICHARD: Wow.

(STEPHANIE *takes his arm.*)

STEPHANIE: What do you think?

RICHARD: I really don't know. My life seems to be turning upside down.

STEPHANIE: That's assuming it was right side up to begin with. You could have been walking all these years with your feet on the ceiling.

RICHARD: Hmm. Yeah. No wonder everything's always looked so confusing.

GLORIA: (*Coming out of the bedroom holding a cell phone*) I just spoke with the minister about the name change, so we should be— (*Seeing* RICHARD) Well, well, well. You look wonderful, Richard.

RICHARD: Thank you.

GLORIA: So? Are we ready?

STEPHANIE: Yes. I think we are.

(STEPHANIE *takes* RICHARD's *arm and they follow* GLORIA *out.)*

Scene 3

(The suite. The next morning. The wedding dress is thrown over a chair, and pieces of the tuxedo and several empty bottles of expensive champagne are scattered across the floor. RICHARD *is passed out on the floor wearing only his boxers.* STEPHANIE *enters, wearing workout gear. She crosses to the bar and begins making herself a drink. He wakes and groans horribly.)*

RICHARD: What's going on? Where am I?

STEPHANIE: You're at the Waldorf. Go back to sleep.

RICHARD: Linda?

STEPHANIE: *(With a sigh)* Stephanie.

RICHARD: Stephanie. *(He sits up and sees her.)* Oh God.

STEPHANIE: Do I look that bad in the morning?

RICHARD: No—no—you look lovely. My head hurts.

STEPHANIE: Bloody Mary?

(RICHARD *groans.)*

STEPHANIE: Best thing for a hangover.

(STEPANIE hands RICHARD *a drink.)*

RICHARD: Thank you. *(He lifts the glass, and notices a wedding ring on his finger.)* Oh God. Are we—?

STEPHANIE: Married? Not legally. We've got to go sign the license this afternoon.

(RICHARD *jumps up and runs into the bathroom, where we hear him vomiting. He returns.)*

STEPHANIE: Are you all right?

RICHARD: I think I have alcohol poisoning.

STEPHANIE: Drink up. It'll help.

RICHARD: How do you know?

STEPHANIE: I went to college.

RICHARD: So did I. But I didn't—uh—party very much. *(He takes a sip of the Bloody Mary.)* Not bad.

STEPHANIE: Where did you go to school?

RICHARD: Ball State. In Indiana, near where I grew up. What about you?

STEPHANIE: Yale for undergrad, and then Columbia for my masters and Ph.D.

RICHARD: Wow. *(Beat)* I started a law degree. But then I realized what I really wanted to do was write—so I dropped out after the first semester...

STEPHANIE: I admire that.

RICHARD: You shouldn't. I haven't done very well.

STEPHANIE: You're making enough to survive in New York.

RICHARD: It's alimony, mostly. Linda is very good at making money.

STEPHANIE: What does she do?

RICHARD: Finance.

STEPHANIE: And how long have you been divorced?

RICHARD: Six months.

STEPHANIE: Uh-oh. That definitely qualifies me as a rebound relationship.

RICHARD: You? What about me? You thought you were marrying somebody else till yesterday morning.

STEPHANIE: That's true.

(Beat)

RICHARD: Did we? —Last night, did we—you know—

STEPHANIE: Consummate the marriage? Several times. And then you threw up in the ice bucket.

RICHARD: Oh God. *(He tries to sit up.)*

STEPHANIE: It's all right. The staff cleaned it up this morning.

(An awkward moment)

STEPHANIE: What will Linda think when she finds out you've gotten married?

RICHARD: I thought you said we weren't married.

STEPHANIE: Well, no, not officially, but you can't back out on me now. Everyone saw us go through with the ceremony.

RICHARD: It's not my fault you got me drunk and then married me!

STEPHANIE: You're a grown man, Richard. You stood up there and said you did, for better or worse, for richer or poorer, etcetera, etcetera, etcetera—

RICHARD: Now you're making me feel like an asshole.

STEPHANIE: Well, you're acting like one! You don't want to sign the license—you call me your ex-wife's name—you throw up all over the hotel room—and you don't even *remember* our wedding night! I should never have married you!

RICHARD: I think we've established that.

STEPHANIE: You're going to walk out on me, aren't you. You're going to let me down just like he did.

RICHARD: No! I mean, yes, I mean—I don't know! I don't know what to do. This is a really fucked-up situation. And okay, maybe it is my fault. And I'm sorry. And I'm especially sorry I don't remember last night because that must have been amazing. I mean, for me. I doubt it would have been all that good for you really. *(Beat)* Linda was the only woman I'd ever been with before.

STEPHANIE: You're kidding.

RICHARD: No. Well, there was an escort...once...right after Linda and I split up. But I think she might have been a man actually.

STEPHANIE: You couldn't tell?

RICHARD: She only gave me a hand job.

STEPHANIE: That doesn't count.

RICHARD: Well, then just Linda. And you.

STEPHANIE: Are you sure there aren't *other* women you don't remember?

RICHARD: No! I mean, yes! I'm sure.

STEPHANIE: Because you were very impressive, actually.

(RICHARD looks at STEPHANIE. The doorbell rings.)

STEPHANIE: That must be Mother. She's supposed to be our witness at City Hall. *(She crosses to the door and opens it.)* Did you forget your key card? —Oh.

(LINDA stands at the door. She has a cast on her wrist.)

LINDA: I'm sorry. I must have the wrong room.

STEPHANIE: Who were you looking for?

LINDA: Richard Lamparsky? The man in the lobby told me he was in 306...

STEPHANIE: Come in. You must be Linda.

LINDA: Yes...

STEPHANIE: Stephanie Winwood. Nice to meet you. Would you like a drink?

LINDA: It's ten in the morning.

STEPHANIE: Yes, but Richard and I have a lot to celebrate.

LINDA: *(Looking behind* STEPHANIE *and seeing* RICHARD*)* Oh, Richard. You *are* here.

RICHARD: Linda. Where were you?

LINDA: There was an accident.

RICHARD: Really?

LINDA: Yes, I was crossing the street and I got hit by a car.

*(*RICHARD *suppresses a startled laugh)*

LINDA: That's not funny!

RICHARD: No—not at all, I'm sorry.

LINDA: I fell down and broke my wrist, and then I had to go to the hospital. And when I got out I tried to call, but your phone wasn't on—

RICHARD: Yeah, I—I turned it off yesterday afternoon.

LINDA: Why did you turn off your phone? *(Taking in the fact that he is shirtless and sitting on the floor)* What's going on here, Richard?

RICHARD: I'm not sure.

LINDA: Is this because I didn't come? Oh, Richard. You had to go hire some cheap— *(Looks at* STEPHANIE*)* — well, very expensive call girl? Where did you get the money for a very expensive call girl anyhow?

*(*GLORIA *enters.)*

GLORIA: Stephanie, sweetheart, are you ready? We're supposed to be there in half an hour.

LINDA: You hired *two* call girls?

GLORIA: Who are you?

LINDA: I'm Linda Martin. Who are you?

GLORIA: Gloria Winwood. You must be the first wife. Richard, you didn't tell me she was so…plain.

LINDA: …*First* wife?

STEPHANIE: Richard and I were married yesterday afternoon.

(Beat)

LINDA: Is that true, Richard?

RICHARD: …More or less. I'm sorry I didn't tell you. It just sort of happened.

LINDA: Getting married does not "just sort of happen"!

STEPHANIE: To men it does.

LINDA: God, Richard. I knew you were hopelessly insensitive, but this takes the cake. The ink on our divorce isn't even dry yet—

RICHARD: *You* were the one that left *me*! In case you've forgotten. You were the one that decided to move to Chicago. You were the one that woke up one morning and realized I wasn't good enough for you any more! Well, guess what? I'm good enough for somebody else now!

(Beat)

LINDA: I should go.

RICHARD: I guess you should.

(LINDA starts to exit.)

RICHARD: Linda—

(LINDA turns.)

RICHARD: I'm sorry…about your wrist.

LINDA: I have a plane to catch.

RICHARD: Okay. Well. Um. Give me a call the next time you're in town.

(LINDA *exits, slamming the door behind her.*)

RICHARD: That's the first time I've ever stood up to her.

STEPHANIE: Congratulations.

RICHARD: Thanks. I—I couldn't have done it if it weren't for you.

STEPHANIE: You owe me one.

RICHARD: I guess I do.

(STEPHANIE *glances meaningfully at his wedding ring.*)

RICHARD: Oh.

GLORIA: Well, come on, Stephanie, you've got to change and we've got to get down there. This isn't like you. We're late for our appointment, this room is a mess, and I'll bet you still haven't packed for Jamaica.

STEPHANIE: I was packed for Jamaica before the wedding. Give us a minute, would you?

(GLORIA *huffs and exits into her bedroom.*)

RICHARD: Jamaica?

STEPHANIE: We'd booked the honeymoon suite at Club Med.

RICHARD: I've never been to Jamaica. Or anywhere tropical, really.

STEPHANIE: You wrote the "Tropical Midnight" series and you've never been anywhere tropical?

RICHARD: There are a lot of things I've written about that I've never done.

STEPHANIE: You ought to.

RICHARD: I can't just rearrange my entire life for someone I just met yesterday!

STEPHANIE: Sir William did.

RICHARD: What?

STEPHANIE: Sir William—your hero. In *Midnight Passion* he decided to follow Lorelei to Maui after he'd known her what—ten minutes?

RICHARD: Actually it was more like five.

STEPHANIE: We've had a whole day longer than that.

(Beat)

RICHARD: I—I have to go—I can't do this—thit's been lovely to meet you, but I have to go home—

STEPHANIE: Home to what? An empty apartment? In a depressing neighborhood? Which you've been too busy missing your ex-wife to clean for the past six months?

RICHARD: Well, yes, but—

STEPHANIE: Wouldn't you rather go to Jamaica?

RICHARD: Yes—I mean of course I would, but—

STEPHANIE: And when you come back, wouldn't you rather live in a penthouse…with me?

RICHARD: I—um—well, yes. I would. But—*married?*

STEPHANIE: Don't you like being married?

RICHARD: Yes, I like being married, I love—well, loved—being married. It made me feel like everything was the way it was supposed to be, like I'd gotten the girl and we were living happily ever after. But then we didn't.

STEPHANIE: Well, now you've got another chance.

RICHARD: But—

STEPHANIE: But what?

(RICHARD can't think of anything else to say.)

STEPHANIE: Will you marry me, Richard?

(RICHARD grabs a bottle of vodka from behind the bar and takes a long drink from it.)

RICHARD: All right.

Scene 4

(A beach in Jamaica. RICHARD and STEPHANIE lie on the sand sipping tropical cocktails. He is writing on a legal pad, and she is simultaneously reading Kant and tapping on her iPhone. He stops writing, looks over, and watches her for a minute.)

RICHARD: What are you working on?

STEPHANIE: This— *(Holding up Kant)* —because I want to expand my dissertation and try to publish. And this— *(Holding up iPhone)* —because now that we're married I want to move out of the Waldorf. There's a place on 72nd that's 63 square feet bigger—but there's a place on 73rd that has a rooftop garden—

RICHARD: Stephanie.

STEPHANIE: What?

RICHARD: You're at the beach, and yet you're simultaneously engaged in two of the world's most challenging activities—reading Kant—is that in the original German?—

STEPHANIE: Yes, of course.

RICHARD: —And trying to find a decent place to live in Manhattan.

STEPHANIE: Do you think we should look in Brooklyn?

RICHARD: No! Well, probably, actually, yeah, but that's not what I'm saying.

STEPHANIE: What are you saying?

RICHARD: I'm saying relax.

STEPHANIE: You're working too.

RICHARD: No, no, I'm just messing around with some notes.

STEPHANIE: For a new book?

RICHARD: Yeah. I haven't written anything in a while—not since Linda left—but I think I've actually got a good idea now.

STEPHANIE: Another "Tropical Midnight" novel?

RICHARD: There can't be any more "Tropical Midnight" novels. Sir William and Lorelei got married.

STEPHANIE: They could always get divorced.

RICHARD: Nobody gets divorced in romance novels.

STEPHANIE: I don't really read many romance novels.

RICHARD: How did you happen to pick up mine, then?

STEPHANIE: Actually Mark was reading them. He had the whole series with him when we met. I'd finished all the books I'd brought, so I asked if I could borrow his…and I thought they were very good, for that kind of thing. What's the new one about?

RICHARD: Oh, you know. Boy meets girl—like all romance novels.

STEPHANIE: Doesn't that get kind of boring?

RICHARD: Well, there's boy meets girl in New York City, but then there's boy meets girl on a tropical island, and that's very different. Or…boy meets girl in the mountains of northern Montana, when she falls off her horse and breaks her leg and he has to carry her a hundred miles to the nearest hospital. But halfway there, girl realizes boy is the evil developer who bought her family's ranch, and she gets so mad she hits him with a piece of firewood and breaks *his* leg.

STEPHANIE: Then how do they get to the hospital?

RICHARD: Well, that's the thing—it's her right leg, and it's his left, so the only way they can walk is to lean on each other. It's a metaphor, see, for the strengths and weaknesses that two people bring to a relationship.

STEPHANIE: You wrote this book, didn't you.

RICHARD: Right after I dropped out of law school. It didn't sell. But the point is, boy meets girl—there's a world of possible stories. They've really only got one thing in common.

STEPHANIE: What's that?

RICHARD: A happy ending.

STEPHANIE: No wonder I don't read many of them.

RICHARD: You don't like happy endings?

STEPHANIE: I just don't find them very convincing. In real life something pretty much always goes wrong. *(Gesturing to his legal pad)* So which variation of boy meets girl is this?

RICHARD: Oh…well, uh, it's sort of about…us, actually. Or people like us. Who meet the way we did.

STEPHANIE: And it's a romance?

(RICHARD nods.)

STEPHANIE: Interesting. *(She looks down at her iPhone)* Oh! I just got an email from our broker. There's a gorgeous penthouse on 75th…but it's only got two and a half bathrooms. Do you think that would be enough?

RICHARD: I think that would be fine. But do we have to figure it out right now?

STEPHANIE: Aren't you concerned about where we're going to live?

RICHARD: Wherever it is, I'm sure it'll be much better than my fifth floor walkup on Avenue C.

STEPHANIE: I'm sure you're right.

RICHARD: So put down the iPhone. Close your eyes and feel the sun on your face.

(STEPHANIE *does.*)

RICHARD: Can I get you another daiquiri?

STEPHANIE: That would be lovely.

(RICHARD *exits.* STEPHANIE *sits with her eyes closed, feeling the sun on her face, until he reenters with two more cocktails.*)

STEPHANIE: You're good for me.

RICHARD: Really?

STEPHANIE: Mm hmm.

RICHARD: Wow…well…thank you—I mean—you're good for me too—

STEPHANIE: I know.

(RICHARD *kisses* STEPHANIE.)

STEPHANIE: I think this might be working out better than I expected.

RICHARD: Me too. *(He kisses her again.)* I needed someone really badly when you came along.

STEPHANIE: You? I was supposed to get married in half an hour.

RICHARD: Yeah.

STEPHANIE: We're lucky. We were both in the right place at the right time.

(RICHARD *leans over and kisses* STEPHANIE *again, and they continue kissing as the lights go down.*)

Scene 5

(Back in New York. STEPHANIE *is alone in the suite at the Waldorf. She sits in an armchair reading Voltaire. The doorbell rings.)*

STEPHANIE: Richard? Did you forget your key card?

*(*STEPHANIE *opens the door. A man [*MARK*] stands there holding an enormous bouquet.)*

STEPHANIE: *Mark?*

MARK: Steffie. Oh, Steffie, oh God, I'm so glad you're here.

*(*MARK *tries to take* STEPHANIE *in his arms, she resists.)*

MARK: I got to New York a week ago, and they told me you were on vacation—I've been calling the desk every day, and as soon as they said you were in I came right over. Here— *(He hands her the bouquet.)* I got you these.

STEPHANIE: *(In a daze)* Thank you. Let me put them in some water.

*(*STEPHANIE *places the flowers in a crystal vase and fills it with water.* MARK *watches her raptly.)*

MARK: You look beautiful, Steffie. You're so tan. Did you go somewhere warm?

STEPHANIE: I went to Jamaica.

MARK: I thought *we* were going to go to Jamaica.

STEPHANIE: So did I.

MARK: Did you go by yourself?

STEPHANIE: I went with my husband.

MARK: Your *what?*

(Beat)

STEPHANIE: What *happened* to you?

MARK: Me? What happened to *you?* You got *married?*

STEPHANIE: I planned a wedding. And I'm not the kind of person to back out of things I've planned.

MARK: Who did you marry?

STEPHANIE: A novelist.

MARK: Had you been seeing him on the side—when you and I were—

STEPHANIE: No.

MARK: Then how—

STEPHANIE: It doesn't matter.

MARK: How could you do this to me?

STEPHANIE: You stood me up for our wedding!

MARK: So you went and married somebody else instead?

STEPHANIE: Of course I did!

MARK: Jesus, Stephanie! (*He grabs the vase and smashes it on the ground. Then he steps through the flowers and broken glass, grabs her, and begins to kiss her passionately.*) You are the most amazing woman I've ever met.

(STEPHANIE *slaps* MARK, *hard. He stumbles backwards and falls, cutting his hands on the glass.*)

STEPHANIE: Are you all right?

MARK: I'm fine.

(MARK *grabs* STEPHANIE *and begins kissing her again, leaving streaks of blood on her shirt. She kisses him back and then pushes him away.*)

STEPHANIE: We can't.

MARK: You're married.

STEPHANIE: You need a doctor.

MARK: I need a blowjob.

(STEPHANIE *slaps* MARK *again.*)

MARK: Jesus, Stephanie!

STEPHANIE: Let me see your hands.

(MARK *holds out his hands, which are still bleeding.*)

MARK: Where's your husband?

STEPHANIE: I sent him to Gucci. He needed new clothes. *(Looking at his hands)* You should go to the emergency room.

MARK: No.

STEPHANIE: You've got pieces of glass sticking out of you!

MARK: So pull them out. Pull them out with your teeth and lick the blood off with your tongue. Heal me.

(STEPHANIE *pulls a sliver of glass out of* MARK's *palm.*)

MARK: Ow!

(STEPHANIE *pulls out another sliver.*)

MARK: OW!

(STEPHANIE *bandages* MARK's *hands.*)

STEPHANIE: There.

MARK: You're incredible.

STEPHANIE: You've gotten blood all over my shirt.

MARK: Take it off.

(STEPHANIE *shrugs and removes her shirt.*)

MARK: God, you're beautiful.

(MARK *picks* STEPHANIE *up and carries her over to the couch. They embrace as the lights go down. Lights come back up on the two of them on the couch in various stages of undress.*)

MARK: That was unbelievable.

STEPHANIE: Yeah, it was nice. Can I get you a drink? *(She stands and crosses to the bar.)*

MARK: Whatever you're having.

(STEPHANIE *pours ice and Grey Goose into two glasses.*)

MARK: I've missed you so much.

STEPHANIE: Where did you go?

MARK: It doesn't matter. I'm here now.

STEPHANIE: It does matter. You're here too late.

MARK: Let's get married.

STEPHANIE: I *am* married.

MARK: So get a divorce and marry me instead.

STEPHANIE: That would look ridiculous. Besides, most people think he *is* you.

(*Off* MARK's *look:*)

STEPHANIE: It's complicated.

MARK: I need you.

STEPHANIE: Where *were* you?

MARK: Vegas.

STEPHANIE: What? (*She pulls away.*) I was crying my eyes out in my ten thousand dollar dress and you were in *Vegas*?

MARK: I got scared. I didn't know if I was ready for this kind of commitment.

STEPHANIE: You should have thought of that before you handed me a ring!

MARK: But you were so amazing, and I got so swept away…and then when you went back home I started to panic—and the day I was going to fly here to meet you I flew to Vegas instead.

STEPHANIE: What did you do there?

MARK: I figured out that you're exactly what I want for the rest of my life.

STEPHANIE: And how did you do that?

MARK: I hired an escort. *(Beat)* I hired a few escorts. *(Beat)* I hired forty escorts and we had a party. Me and the escorts. It lasted all night. And at one point around four a.m. I had three of them and they were all, you know, doing different things to me, and I kept looking back and forth between these escorts and all I could see was your face.

STEPHANIE: I don't believe this.

MARK: No, Steffie, listen. The most beautiful escorts in Vegas…huge, naked tits bouncing in my face…hot, wet tongues licking my…you get the idea. The point is, all I could think about was you. And that's when I realized how much I loved you. How I didn't want anyone else—at least not very often. So here I am.

(Beat)

STEPHANIE: You should go.

MARK: No, Steffie, please. I'll never go to an escort again—I'll never even look at an escort—I'll never even look at a regular woman! I love you so much!

STEPHANIE: It's too late.

MARK: But don't you love me?

STEPHANIE: No.

MARK: Then why did you say we should get married?

STEPHANIE: It seemed like a good idea at the time.

MARK: What?

STEPHANIE: There's a big difference between loving somebody and marrying them.

MARK: There shouldn't be!

STEPHANIE: Maybe not, but there is.

MARK: If you won't marry me I'll join a monastery. I'll shave off all my hair and join a monastery in Thailand.

STEPHANIE: Send me a postcard.

MARK: I'll send you my ear!

STEPHANIE: That's not very original.

MARK: Steffie, please!

STEPHANIE: Mark, I'm already married. Very happily, as a matter of fact, and I'm planning to stay that way.

(The sound of a key card in the lock.)

STEPHANIE: That's probably him right now.

(The door opens. RICHARD enters carrying shopping bags.)

STEPHANIE: Hi, Richard. This is Mark.

RICHARD: *(Taken aback)* Oh.

STEPHANIE: Mark, this is my husband, Richard.

RICHARD: Nice to…meet you.

STEPHANIE: Mark was just leaving.

(MARK falls to his knees and clutches STEPHANIE's feet.)

STEPHANIE: Richard, could you call security? It's speed dial two.

(RICHARD goes to the phone and dials.)

RICHARD: Hi—it's Richard Lamparsky.

MARK: *(Looking up)* Richard Lamparsky? You wrote the "Tropical Midnight" series.

RICHARD: Yeah…

MARK: Those were great!

RICHARD: Oh. Wow, thanks.

MARK: Are you working on anything new?

RICHARD: I, uh—yeah, I am, actually.

MARK: I can't wait. Hey, do you think you could sign my copies if I brought them by sometime?

RICHARD: Sure, yeah, I'd be happy—

STEPHANIE: *(To* MARK*)* I'd really suggest you go, unless you feel like being arrested.

MARK: All right. All right, I'll go—but I'll be back, Steffie. This isn't the end of this. *(To* RICHARD*)* It was so great to meet you. *(He exits.)*

RICHARD: Why are you in your bra?

STEPHANIE: I got blood on my shirt.

RICHARD: Are you hurt? Should I call—?

STEPHANIE: No, no, I'm fine. It was his blood, not mine.

RICHARD: What happened? Did he—did he try to—? *(He is about to charge down the hall after* MARK.*)*

STEPHANIE: No, no—it was totally consensual.

(Beat)

RICHARD: What?

STEPHANIE: I think we should probably be open about our affairs, don't you?

RICHARD: *Our* affairs?

STEPHANIE: Well, mine, so far, I guess.

RICHARD: Are there others?

STEPHANIE: Not yet. But there probably will be. *(Beat)* I'm sorry. Maybe we should have gotten this out up front.

RICHARD: Um. I mean maybe I should have assumed it—because of our circumstances—

STEPHANIE: Well, it's not as though we're in love or something like that.

(Beat)

RICHARD: No.

STEPHANIE: But it isn't you.

RICHARD: You mean you'd...cheat on anybody?

STEPHANIE: I think everyone does.

RICHARD: No they don't! Linda and I were married for eighteen years and neither of us ever -

STEPHANIE: Are you sure? Because that's what my mother thought.

RICHARD: Your father—

STEPHANIE: Yes, for years. Mother never knew until she caught him in the act, and then they fought, and then he told her he was leaving.

RICHARD: How old were you?

STEPHANIE: Fifteen.

RICHARD: I'm sorry.

STEPHANIE: It's all right. He taught me a lot.

RICHARD: I can see that!

(Beat)

STEPHANIE: What did you get at Gucci?

RICHARD: I don't know. Pants. Stephanie—

(STEPHANIE opens the bag and holds up a pair of dress pants.)

STEPHANIE: Oh, they're lovely. Your choice of first wife notwithstanding, I thought you might have good taste.

RICHARD: Stephanie, I don't see how I can be with—

STEPHANIE: Richard, we live in a world of options. It's unrealistic to try to limit ourselves to—

(GLORIA enters, carrying shopping bags.)

GLORIA: Hello, sweetheart. Richard.

STEPHANIE: Mother. I thought you had dinner plans.

GLORIA: I did.

STEPHANIE: And?

GLORIA: Ralph canceled. *(She sets her bags down, crosses to the bar, and begins mixing drinks.)* Permanently. Apparently he's met a younger woman and they've fallen in love. Martini?

STEPHANIE: Yes, thank you.

GLORIA: Richard?

RICHARD: Sure. I—uh—I'm sorry about Ralph.

GLORIA: Oh, don't be. I had a perfectly nice day. I went to Bergdorf's and bought myself a bracelet, and then I had three of these lovely things *(Indicating martini)* on the way home. Stephanie, sweetheart, why are you in your bra?

STEPHANIE: It's a long story.

RICHARD: Stephanie, can we talk?

STEPHANIE: No, I'm sorry, I can't right now. I've got a nail appointment downtown. *(She sets her martini glass down, crosses to the closet and takes out a jacket.)*

RICHARD: Well, try not to sleep with anybody on the way home.

(STEPHANIE puts on the jacket and exits, slamming the door behind her. A pause. GLORIA downs half of her martini in one gulp.)

GLORIA: Ah, newlyweds.

(RICHARD, martini glass in hand, begins to exit.)

GLORIA: Where are you going?

RICHARD: Oh—I was just going to—go to my room.

GLORIA: Why?

RICHARD: I—uh, well—I have to pack, actually.

GLORIA: Pack for what?

(RICHARD *is silent.*)

GLORIA: You don't mean you're leaving?

RICHARD: I think I have to. I mean, I can't stay—not like this—

GLORIA: Not like what? What happened?

(*Beat*)

RICHARD: Nothing.

GLORIA: Richard, I'm Stephanie's mother. I know her better than anyone in the world. If there's anybody you ought to talk to, it's certainly me.

(RICHARD *takes a large gulp of his martini.*)

RICHARD: Stephanie and I—in Jamaica—we were talking about happy endings.

GLORIA: You mean for massages?

RICHARD: No! I mean for books. For romance novels.

GLORIA: I don't read many romance novels.

RICHARD: There's sort of a formula. Boy meets girl, boy and girl fall in love, and then boy and girl get married. And Stephanie said that in real life, something always goes wrong.

GLORIA: Of course it does. In real life, even if boy and girl make it to the altar—which is unlikely enough— that's hardly the end of the love story. Maybe it was in the past—people got married, and then they stayed married—but today more than half of them get divorced.

RICHARD: True.

GLORIA: So maybe a few years later, boy cheats on girl with his secretary, and then he leaves her—or she leaves him. And she goes to Florida and has the time of her life with some pretty young pool boy—but then *he* leaves her, or he cheats on her with her best friend, or he gets lymphoma, or sarcoma, or multiple myeloma. And then a few years after that, girl has a stroke and dies alone in a nursing home with Cream of Wheat dribbling down her chin. And *that's* the end of the love story.

RICHARD: That's terrible.

GLORIA: I guess so, if you think too much about it.

RICHARD: How do you keep from thinking too much about it?

GLORIA: Well…what I do is I have a lot of sex. And I suppose what *you* do is you write stories which end at the right time.

(Beat)

RICHARD: Stephanie slept with Mark.

GLORIA: I see.

RICHARD: And I'm sure she's still in love with him, and so I ought to just go—

GLORIA: Oh, no, she was never in love with Mark.

RICHARD: Then why did she want to marry him?

GLORIA: She was ready to get married…and there he was. I hear he's very handsome—she may have been infatuated with him—but I'm sure it didn't go beyond that.

RICHARD: I'd settle for infatuation.

GLORIA: I'm afraid you're not the sort of man with whom a girl like Stephanie becomes infatuated. I think it would take a more…mature woman to be smitten with your obvious qualities. *(Beat)* Stephanie's broken dozens of hearts. Just like I used to do in my time. I was even lovelier than Stephanie when I was young, would you believe it?

RICHARD: *(Looking at her)* Yes.

GLORIA: You're so sweet. If I were her I don't know how I'd be able to resist you.

RICHARD: Oh—well—

GLORIA: And you've got a marvelous body—do you work out?

RICHARD: Yes, I—I try to.

GLORIA: Wonderful. I think it's important to take care of our bodies, don't you?

RICHARD: Yes.

GLORIA: A healthy diet, regular exercise...of course, there are all kinds of exercise. I prefer to take mine outside the gym. *(She pours herself another martini.)* Another?

RICHARD: All right.

(GLORIA pours RICHARD another martini as well.)

GLORIA: Cheers.

RICHARD: Cheers.

GLORIA: First all that trouble with your former wife—though what you saw in her I'll never know—and then you had to go and get involved with a girl like Stephanie.

RICHARD: Well, it wasn't my idea to marry her.

GLORIA: No. It was mine, wasn't it.

RICHARD: So I guess that means this whole thing is your fault.

GLORIA: I guess it does. *(Beat)* Is there something I might be able to do to make up for it?

RICHARD: I...don't know.

GLORIA: Would you like to find out?

(GLORIA *leans towards* RICHARD, *and they kiss. She pulls away.*)

GLORIA: Did you say you were going to your room?

RICHARD: Yes—I'll do that—I'm sorry, I don't know what I was thinking, I— *(She leans forward and kisses him again.)* Would you like to come with me?

END OF ACT ONE

ACT TWO

Scene 1

(RICHARD *and* STEPHANIE *in the suite. Later that evening.*)

STEPHANIE: You *what*?

RICHARD: Listen, Stephanie, if I'd known it was going to upset you—

STEPHANIE: You fucked my mother!

RICHARD: Your mother and I…made love…

STEPHANIE: My mother does not make love. My mother fucks.

(RICHARD *considers.*)

RICHARD: That's true.

STEPHANIE: How many times did you do it?

(*Beat*)

RICHARD: Seven.

STEPHANIE: In two hours?

RICHARD: Your mother is…quite amazing.

STEPHANIE: Is she better than me?

RICHARD: What?

STEPHANIE: Is she better in bed than I am?

RICHARD: No! Stephanie, of course not.

STEPHANIE: Tell me the truth.

RICHARD: Yes. But that's only natural, she's had *much* more experience.

STEPHANIE: God! We've been married two weeks and you've cheated on me seven times already!

RICHARD: You can't count like that!

STEPHANIE: Oh really? Are you a cheating expert?

RICHARD: Of course not! You're the one who cheated on me first!

STEPHANIE: Then who are you to say how you can count?

RICHARD: Seven times would mean with seven different people.

STEPHANIE: So now that you've counted my mother, you can sleep with her as much as you like?

RICHARD: I don't like! Well, I did like. But I won't like again. I don't think.

STEPHANIE: You don't *think*?

RICHARD: You told me we ought to have affairs. You told me we ought to be up front about them.

STEPHANIE: I know. *(Beat)* Mother and I have been competing for men since I was fifteen years old.

RICHARD: Really?

STEPHANIE: Are you surprised?

RICHARD: Well. No. I guess I'm not. I'm just…surprised that you're competing for *me.*

STEPHANIE: Yes, that is odd, isn't it.

RICHARD: Well, it isn't *that* odd. Is it?

STEPHANIE: You can't really expect me to compliment you right now.

(GLORIA *enters.*)

GLORIA: Stephanie, sweetheart, you'll never guess who I slept with.

STEPHANIE: My husband.

GLORIA: Well, yes. But also the most amazing bartender.

RICHARD: You did?

GLORIA: Who wants a brandy?

STEPHANIE: I think I need one right now.

RICHARD: Me too.

GLORIA: *(Crossing to the bar, pouring drinks)* I went out to a late dinner with Aunt Myrna, and…mmmm. Let's just say I didn't need to order dessert.

STEPHANIE: Have you told anyone else about you and Richard?

GLORIA: No, sweetheart, I think it's best to keep these things in the family. Anyone else might not understand.

STEPHANIE: Did it occur to you that *I* might not understand?

GLORIA: You don't mean to tell me you're angry. It's not as though you're in love or something like that.

STEPHANIE: No.

GLORIA: I was trying to do you a favor. Though I can't say I didn't enjoy myself—that husband of yours is a tiger in bed.

STEPHANIE: How does seducing my husband qualify as a favor?

GLORIA: He was thinking of leaving, which would obviously be inconvenient for everyone.

STEPHANIE: *(To* RICHARD*)* You were?

RICHARD: That's actually what I wanted to talk to you about. But we kind of got stuck at the part where I—well, you know.

GLORIA: I figured I'd stall him. Maybe even make him change his mind.

RICHARD: You did?

GLORIA: You thought I just couldn't resist you?

RICHARD: Something like that.

GLORIA: *(To* STEPHANIE*)* Men *are* funny, aren't they, sweetheart?

RICHARD: You told me you had a great time.

GLORIA: I did.

RICHARD: You told me we ought to do it again later.

STEPHANIE: You did?

GLORIA: Of course we won't, if you'd rather we didn't.

(Beat)

STEPHANIE: Are you still thinking of leaving, Richard?

RICHARD: I don't—I don't know.

STEPHANIE: Because I really think we should stay married.

RICHARD: You do?

STEPHANIE: Don't you?

RICHARD: I want to. But I don't see how I can—

STEPHANIE: Can what? Live in a gorgeous apartment? With a beautiful woman? And also be free to sleep with other beautiful women whenever you like?

RICHARD: Well, yes, but—

STEPHANIE: It's sort of an ideal situation, don't you think?

RICHARD: Well—yes, it sounds—it seems like it's ideal, but—

STEPHANIE: But what?

(RICHARD *can't think of anything to say.*)

STEPHANIE: Will you try?

RICHARD: All right.

STEPHANIE: Good. (*Briskly*) Then, if you'll excuse me, I have a call to make. (*She takes out her phone and dials. As she closes her bedroom door*) Mark?

(RICHARD *looks from the door back to* GLORIA.)

RICHARD: That wasn't the way that was supposed to go.

GLORIA: Well, things rarely go the way they're supposed to, do they. Care for another drink?

RICHARD: Sure.

(GLORIA *crosses to the bar and pours two more brandies.*)

GLORIA: I have a feeling you're not going to be sleeping in there tonight.

(GLORIA *hands* RICHARD *a brandy and runs a finger down his chest.*)

GLORIA: Wherever will you sleep instead?

(GLORIA *and* RICHARD *begin to kiss.*)

RICHARD: You and your daughter are the most unconventional women I've ever met.

GLORIA: We can afford to be.

(*Still kissing,* GLORIA *and* RICHARD *make their way into her bedroom.*)

Scene 2

(The next morning. The sounds of vigorous sex from behind both bedroom doors. After a few moments, STEPHANIE's door opens and she emerges, followed by MARK.)

MARK: God, Steffie, I was so happy when you called. I knew you wanted to be with me. I knew you'd give me another chance. We'll just get your marriage taken care of—I know a great divorce lawyer—and then we can—

(GLORIA's door opens and she emerges, followed by RICHARD. He is wearing his new pants.)

MARK: Oh! Hello. *(Recognizing RICHARD, to STEPHANIE)* That's—

STEPHANIE: My husband. Yes. And this is my mother.

(MARK is dumbfounded.)

STEPHANIE: Mother, this is Mark.

GLORIA: Close your mouth, dear, that's a good boy.

(MARK does.)

GLORIA: It's a pleasure to make your acquaintance. *(She goes into the kitchen and pours herself a bowl of cereal.)*

MARK: Oh, Steffie, the lawyer is going to have a field day with this one—

STEPHANIE: I'm not getting divorced, Mark.

MARK: You're...not?

STEPHANIE: Richard and I have an agreement. Martini?

MARK: It's ten in the morning.

STEPHANIE: Bloody Mary? *(She goes behind the bar and begins mixing a drink.)*

MARK: No.

STEPHANIE: Good, because I'm using the last of the vodka.

GLORIA: Oh dear. What kind of wine do you think would go with cornflakes?

STEPHANIE: Try the '98 Montrachet.

GLORIA: Richard?

RICHARD: Sure.

MARK: Steffie, this—this—this is obscene!

STEPHANIE: And a party with forty escorts isn't?

MARK: Steffie, everyone makes mistakes, but—

STEPHANIE: I don't.

MARK: If you don't walk out that door with me right now you're making the biggest mistake of your life!

RICHARD: Excuse me?

MARK: What?

RICHARD: Stephanie is my wife and she's not walking out the door with anyone.

MARK: But you're fucking her mother!

RICHARD: That's a completely separate issue.

MARK: I'm not just going to stand by and let you treat the woman I love like that!

RICHARD: How do you think she's treating me?

MARK: Better than you deserve, I'm sure!

RICHARD: I think you'd better go.

MARK: I think you'd better make me!

RICHARD: You want me to?

MARK: Just try it. I'll kick your ass back to the tropical island you came from.

RICHARD: I came from the Lower East Side. I've never even been to a tropical island—well, except Jamaica—

MARK: Really? Man, you've got a great imagination.

RICHARD: Thanks! I—I did a lot of research online.

(For a moment it is unclear whether they will fight or carry on with the conversation. Then MARK *lunges for* RICHARD *and they roll on the ground, kicking and punching.* STEPHANIE *and* GLORIA *watch them.)*

GLORIA: My goodness, sweetheart, Mark is certainly...

STEPHANIE: Don't even think about it.

(The doorbell rings.)

GLORIA: Are we expecting anyone?

STEPHANIE: I'm not. Are you?

GLORIA: No. I have an appointment with one of the porters— *(Checking her watch)* —but not until three.

(The doorbell again. STEPHANIE *opens the door a crack.* LINDA *stands outside. She still has a cast on her wrist, and she is also wearing a neck brace.)*

LINDA: Is Richard here?

STEPHANIE: Yes.

LINDA: Could I talk to him for a minute?

*(*STEPHANIE *opens the door and* LINDA *steps inside to see* RICHARD *and* MARK *punching and kicking each other on the floor.)*

LINDA: Good God, Richard, what do you think you're doing!

*(*RICHARD *looks up.)*

RICHARD: Linda!

*(*MARK *hits* RICHARD *with a sucker punch, and* RICHARD *goes down hard. He lies on the carpet, unconscious.)*

LINDA: Richard!

STEPHANIE: Richard!

(Both LINDA *and* STEPHANIE *hurry over to* RICHARD's *prone body.* GLORIA *sips her wine and eyes* MARK *speculatively.)*

MARK: Steffie?

STEPHANIE: *(Dabbing at a cut on* RICHARD's *forehead)* Richard, are you all right?

LINDA: *(Slapping* RICHARD's *face)* Richard, wake up, Richard!

STEPHANIE: Don't do that! —He might have a concussion. *(She crosses to the bar to grab a bottle of brandy.)*

MARK: My hand hurts too, you know!

STEPHANIE: *(To* MARK) Will you shut up!

*(*MARK *stares at* STEPHANIE *in shock for a moment, then breaks into sobs.* GLORIA *crosses to* MARK *and strokes his arm.)*

GLORIA: There, there. You poor boy.

*(*STEPHANIE *holds the brandy to* RICHARD's *lips.)*

LINDA: I don't think this is the right time for Richard to be drinking!—

*(*RICHARD *coughs, sputters, and wakes up.)*

RICHARD: I—what—Linda? Stephanie?

STEPHANIE: Have some more brandy, Richard.

*(*RICHARD *takes another swallow of brandy.)*

RICHARD: What happened?

LINDA: A strange man hit you.

RICHARD: *(Trying to sit up)* Where is he? I'll kill him—

*(*RICHARD *sees* MARK, *who is still sobbing.)*

RICHARD: Oh. Is—uh—is everything all right?

MARK: *(Sobbing)* No!

GLORIA: You know what you need?

MARK: What?

GLORIA: A drink.

STEPHANIE: I think we all do.

(GLORIA *takes the brandy bottle from* RICHARD. MARK *grabs the bottle from her and drinks deeply from it.*)

MARK: You were right. (*He drinks again.*) I feel better already.

GLORIA: Of course you do. It's the best thing for a broken heart.

(GLORIA *takes the bottle and drinks herself, then passes it to* STEPHANIE, *and* STEPHANIE *passes it to* RICHARD, *still lying on the floor. They continue passing the bottle between them,* MARK *drinking the most.*)

RICHARD: Can I—can we—offer you some brandy, Linda?

LINDA: No.

RICHARD: I'm sure there are some glasses… somewhere…

LINDA: You never used to drink.

RICHARD: I know. Just think what I was missing.

LINDA: You never used to dress like that, either.

STEPHANIE: They're nice, aren't they?

LINDA: They look very expensive.

STEPHANIE: They were.

RICHARD: So…Linda…how are you?

LINDA: Just fine. Very busy. And you?

RICHARD: Well, my head hurts, and I think I'm turning into a terrible person. But other than that I guess I'm doing all right. What happened to your neck?

LINDA: There was an accident.

RICHARD: Really?

LINDA: Yes, I was on my way to the airport and I got hit by a bus.

(RICHARD *suppresses a startled laugh.*)

LINDA: That's not funny!

RICHARD: No. No, of course not.

LINDA: If it hadn't happened I would have been here yesterday.

RICHARD: Oh. Well. What brings you to town?

LINDA: I need to talk to you, Richard.

RICHARD: Um. Okay. About what?

LINDA: I've got some good news.

RICHARD: Yes?

LINDA: I think we should get back together.

(RICHARD *coughs and sputters, spitting a mouthful of brandy onto the floor.*)

RICHARD: You what?

LINDA: I flew into town because I wanted to tell you in person.

RICHARD: Linda…I'm married.

LINDA: Yes, I know, and it was very insensitive of you. You can use my divorce lawyer. He's much better than yours was.

MARK: *(Hopefully)* You're getting divorced?

STEPHANIE: No, I'm not. And neither is Richard.

(MARK *begins to sob again.*)

GLORIA: *(Whispering to* STEPHANIE*)* I'll just take care of him for you.

MARK: Steffie, I'll never look at another woman again…

GLORIA: There, there. It's all right. *(She strokes his shoulder, then moves her hand down to his thigh.)* You know—you have a marvelous body.

MARK: *(Through his tears)* I—I try to work out.

GLORIA: It shows.

MARK: It does?

GLORIA: Mm hmm. And you have such nice lips, too.

MARK: I do?

GLORIA: Mm hmm. Tell me, are they as soft as they look? *(She leans in to kiss him.)*

LINDA: Who is that man?

STEPHANIE: My ex-fiance.

(LINDA looks back and forth between them, confused. MARK picks GLORIA up and carries her into her bedroom.)

LINDA: Well…Richard, should we go?

(RICHARD doesn't move.)

LINDA: Do you need to pack?

(Beat)

RICHARD: I—

LINDA: *(Looking around the lavish suite.)* Oh, Richard. It's all this, isn't it. I'm so disappointed in you.

RICHARD: Why?

LINDA: You're drinking. You're living in a penthouse. You're wearing expensive clothes. You're sleeping with a beautiful woman.

RICHARD: *(Muttered)* Two.

(STEPHANIE sighs.)

LINDA: What?

RICHARD: Nothing.

LINDA: And you've let yourself think all that will make you happier than being with the woman you really love.

RICHARD: No, it's not that—

LINDA: Richard, we've loved each other since we were eighteen!

RICHARD: I know.

LINDA: Freshman year of college.

RICHARD: The first week—

LINDA: In the cafeteria.

RICHARD: I noticed you from across the room.

LINDA: It would have been hard not to—we were the only ones at breakfast.

RICHARD: That's right—everyone else was still hung over from the night before. But even if it had been full I would have noticed you anyway. You were eating eggs—

LINDA: No I wasn't, I was eating pancakes.

RICHARD: Oh that's right, it was pancakes—blueberry pancakes.

LINDA: And you were eating cereal. And you were too shy to come and sit with me—

RICHARD: I came and sat with you.

LINDA: No you didn't—I had to carry my tray across the room and ask if I could sit down.

RICHARD: Well, I was glad when you did.

(LINDA *and* RICHARD *smile at each other, lost in recollection.* MARK, *from inside the bedroom, moans loudly. All three of them look over, then return to their conversation.)*

LINDA: When we got divorced, do you remember what you told me?

RICHARD: I love you? …I can't live without you? …I'm going to jump off the Brooklyn Bridge?

LINDA: Well, yes, but what else?

RICHARD: I'm not sure.

LINDA: You told me nobody ever gets divorced in romance novels.

RICHARD: Oh, right.

LINDA: And…I was hoping…maybe nobody's ever too late in romance novels either.

RICHARD: No. Everybody in romance novels is always in the right place at the right time.

(MARK *moans again. They look towards the bedroom, then turn back.)*

RICHARD: Do you remember what you told *me?* You told me you didn't love me anymore.

LINDA: I was wrong. I still love you. I've always loved you.

STEPHANIE: She's lying.

LINDA: No I'm not!

STEPHANIE: You say you love him, but what you mean is you think he's the best you can do. You thought there was something better out there, and you looked around for a while and found out there isn't—at least not for a middle-aged divorcee with bad shoes. So you decided you ought to settle for what you could get.

LINDA: Richard, don't listen to her! I know you—and I know that however many penthouses you have, you can't be happy without love in your life.

RICHARD: You're right. But you don't really love me. And I don't love you either, not anymore.

LINDA: But you've been waiting for me to take you back since we got divorced!

RICHARD: I know. You've got terrible timing. (*Indicating brandy*) You sure I can't offer you some of this?

(LINDA *grabs the bottle of brandy and drinks deeply.*)

LINDA: Are you trying to tell me you've actually fallen for *her*?

RICHARD: Well, uh, now that you mention it—

STEPHANIE: What?

RICHARD: Stephanie, listen. I haven't dared to say this…haven't really even dared to think it…but now that I see Linda again I realize that the way I used to feel about her—I don't—I feel that way about you now.

(MARK *moans loudly a third time.*)

RICHARD: Do you think you could keep it down in there? I—I'm trying to declare my love to your daughter.

GLORIA: Oh, really? We wouldn't want to miss that.

(*A moment later, hair disheveled, she emerges from the bedroom.* MARK *follows, tugging at her sleeve. To* MARK:)

GLORIA: We'll carry on in a moment.

RICHARD: Well—uh—okay.

(RICHARD *grabs the bottle of brandy from* LINDA *and drinks deeply. She snatches it back. He takes* STEPHANIE's *hand.*)

RICHARD: Stephanie, I—I love the way you read Kant—in German—on the beach. I love the way you know which wine to serve with *breakfast.* I love the way you look in a bikini. I love the way you look in sweats, curled up in that chair. I love the way you look in the middle of the night when the moon comes through the window and turns your eyelashes silver.

MARK: Oh, he's good.

STEPHANIE: I think that's the loveliest thing that anyone's ever said to me.

LINDA: I'm going to throw up. *(She runs into the bathroom, where we hear her vomiting.)*

RICHARD: Linda's not much of a drinker.

(LINDA returns.)

RICHARD: Are you all right?

LINDA: I—I should go.

RICHARD: Oh. Okay. Well. Um. Thanks for stopping by.

LINDA: She doesn't love you, Richard. She doesn't even know you—and you don't know her. You're just a hopeless romantic who'd fall for any girl who gave you the time of day, and nobody else ever has before. And when this all falls apart, I hope you don't expect to come running back to me. *(She starts to exit.)*

RICHARD: Linda—

LINDA: Yes?

RICHARD: Are you going to be all right?

LINDA: I'm going to be fine. *(She starts to exit again.)*

RICHARD: Linda?

LINDA: Yes?

RICHARD: I'm sorry…about your neck.

LINDA: I have a plane to catch.

RICHARD: Okay. Goodbye, Linda.

(LINDA exits.)

STEPHANIE: Richard, I—I mean—we had an agreement.

RICHARD: I don't want an agreement. Maybe I am just a hopeless romantic—but I want love in my life. And I don't want to sleep with your mother—

GLORIA: Excuse me?

RICHARD: And I don't want you to sleep with Mark—or anyone else.

MARK: Hey!

RICHARD: I want to have you and hold you and love you and cherish you till death do us part.

STEPHANIE: You're asking too much! You're sitting in a penthouse suite at the Waldorf Astoria! You're drinking Hennessy! You're wearing Gucci pants! You can go anywhere in the world—in a private jet!

RICHARD: We have a private jet?

STEPHANIE: Of course.

RICHARD: Why didn't we take it to Jamaica?

STEPHANIE: It was being redecorated. I didn't tell you?

RICHARD: No.

STEPHANIE: Sorry.

RICHARD: It doesn't matter. *(Beat)* What Linda and I used to have—I didn't care where I was as long as she was there. And when she wasn't, I could be anywhere in the world and it wouldn't be any good without her.

STEPHANIE: Didn't that scare you?

RICHARD: No—because I believe in happy endings. I know I didn't get one the first time around, but I still believe someday I will. I doubted it for a while, but you've brought this feeling, this love back into my heart, and it feels too good for me to believe it won't end somewhere wonderful. I know we haven't known each other long, and I know it's probably crazy to think a girl like you would ever fall for someone like me— but I wonder if maybe eventually you might be able to love me too.

(Beat)

STEPHANIE: No.

(Beat)

RICHARD: I see.

STEPHANIE: Richard, listen. Maybe I can't be absolutely everything you want, but nobody can. Being happy is about learning how to live with what you have—and we have a good life here.

RICHARD: It's not good enough. I want something perfect. I'm forty years old and I'm divorced and I'm losing my hair and I ought to know better, but I want something perfect.

STEPHANIE: There's no such thing. So we learn to settle for what we can get.

RICHARD: I don't want to settle for what I can get. *(Beat)* I'm leaving.

(MARK looks up.)

STEPHANIE: Richard—

RICHARD: If you can't love me, then I can't stay.

STEPHANIE: So you want to walk out on me—abandon me…

RICHARD: Uh, I guess that's one way to put it.

STEPHANIE: And what am I supposed to do?

MARK: I'll marry you, Steffie!

STEPHANIE: Oh, God.

GLORIA: You know, sweetheart…hardly anyone would know the difference.

STEPHANIE: But—

GLORIA: Hardly anyone's met Richard.

STEPHANIE: They met him at the wedding.

GLORIA: They saw him from a distance, but then he drank so much champagne that he spent the reception vomiting in the bathroom.

RICHARD: I did?

(GLORIA *nods.*)

RICHARD: Sorry.

GLORIA: We'll just tell them Mark is your legal name.

MARK: Let's get married, Steffie!

STEPHANIE: I wouldn't trust you to show up.

MARK: Oh, Steffie, you know I would! You know I've learned my lesson. I love you so much. *(Beat)* Only— would you mind too much if occasionally—your mother and I...

STEPHANIE: *(To* GLORIA*)* You have a remarkable effect on men.

GLORIA: Sweetheart, this is really the most practical solution. And he'll look much better on the Christmas cards than Richard would have.

(RICHARD *thinks about being offended, then looks at* MARK *and concedes the point.* MARK *gets down on one knee and takes* STEPHANIE'*s hand.*)

MARK: Will you marry me, Steffie?

(STEPHANIE *sighs.*)

STEPHANIE: All right.

MARK: Oh, Steffie, I'm so...happy...

(MARK *stumbles, sways drunkenly and then passes out. Beat)*

RICHARD: Well. Now that that's...settled, I guess I'll be going.

STEPHANIE: All right.

RICHARD: All right. *(Beat)* I'll miss you.

STEPHANIE: I'll have your things sent back to your place.

RICHARD: Thanks. *(Beat)* Goodbye, Gloria. You've been—well—there are no words.

GLORIA: *(Pleased)* Thank you, Richard. *(Looking at* MARK's *prone body)* I hate it when men get me all worked up and then pass out. I suppose I'll have to call that porter and tell him to come up early. *(She exits into her bedroom.)*

RICHARD: So…I should go.

STEPHANIE: All right.

RICHARD: All right. I'll go. I'm…going to go.

*(*RICHARD *begins to exit. As he is almost out the door:)*

STEPHANIE: Richard—

RICHARD: Yes?

STEPHANIE: Are you going to be okay?

RICHARD: I'm going to be miserable.

STEPHANIE: Then you should stay.

RICHARD: I…can't.

STEPHANIE: Well. I hope you find what you're looking for.

RICHARD: Thank you. *(Beat)* It was a great honeymoon.

STEPHANIE: It was. We were really happy, weren't we.

RICHARD: Yeah, for about two weeks.

STEPHANIE: That's probably about as long as most married couples are happy.

RICHARD: You're probably right.

*(*RICHARD *turns and begins to exit. As he is almost out the door:)*

STEPHANIE: Richard—

RICHARD: Yes?

STEPHANIE: What about the book?

RICHARD: What book?

STEPHANIE: The one you're writing—you know—about us.

RICHARD: What about it?

STEPHANIE: How's it going to end now?

RICHARD: Oh. *(Beat)* Well. He'll probably tell her... something like what I told you. And she'll probably tell him something...like what you told me. And he'll tell her that if that's the way it is then he's leaving. And just as he's almost out the door...she'll call after him— just like you did, just now. And she'll tell him that even though she's scared...she knows he loves her—and deep down she knows she might be able to love him too. And he'll go to her, and he'll take her in his arms and they'll kiss. *(Beat)* It'll probably end something like that.

STEPHANIE: *(Softly)* That's a nice ending.

(RICHARD *and* STEPHANIE *look at each other, as the lights slowly go down.)*

END OF PLAY

www.ingramcontent.com/pod-product-compliance
Lightning Source LLC
Chambersburg PA
CBHW070028110426
42741CB00034B/2681